Love in Bloom

Love in Bloom

Matthew Petchinsky

Love in Bloom: 5-Minute Romantic Gestures
By: Matthew Petchinsky

Introduction: The Art of Expressing Love in Small but Meaningful Ways

Love is often regarded as the grandest of emotions, capable of moving mountains, healing wounds, and transforming lives. Yet, for all its magnitude, love's most profound expressions are often found not in grand gestures or monumental sacrifices but in the small, thoughtful actions that quietly affirm our care and devotion. This truth transcends romantic relationships, extending to friendships, familial bonds, and even the way we treat ourselves.

In a world often consumed by hustle and spectacle, the understated power of meaningful gestures can be a balm to the heart. Small acts of love have a unique ability to create lasting impact because they are personal, intentional, and consistent. A simple note left on the bathroom mirror, an unexpected hug, or a perfectly brewed cup of coffee just the way someone likes it—all these are everyday expressions of love that speak volumes without uttering a word.

This guide is an invitation to rediscover the beauty of simplicity in expressing love. It is not about how much time, money, or resources you can invest but rather about how you can use creativity, thoughtfulness, and presence to communicate what words sometimes cannot. Whether you are looking to nurture your relationship with a partner, deepen your bond with family, or even foster self-love, the suggestions in this guide will offer a treasure trove of inspiration.

Why Small Gestures Matter

Small, meaningful expressions of love are the unsung heroes of relationships. They are the glue that holds connections together during life's inevitable ups and downs. Unlike grand declarations that can sometimes feel overwhelming or even obligatory, small acts of love are genuine, spontaneous, and often unexpected.

Psychologists have long recognized the importance of what is often called "micro-affections"—the little things we do to show we care. These seemingly minor acts serve to build trust, foster emotional intimacy, and remind others that they are valued. They create a sense of security and belonging, which are foundational to any healthy relationship.

Barriers to Expressing Love

Despite our best intentions, expressing love in meaningful ways is not always easy. Busy schedules, misunderstandings, and even our upbringing can create barriers to showing affection. For instance, some people may feel unsure about how to express their feelings or may worry that their efforts won't be appreciated. Others may find themselves caught in the misconception that love must always be demonstrated through dramatic or expensive gestures.

This guide aims to break down these barriers by offering practical tips and examples that fit seamlessly into everyday life. You'll learn how to observe and understand the unique ways your loved ones receive affection and how to tailor your gestures to align with their preferences.

What You Will Learn

This guide is divided into practical, actionable sections designed to help you incorporate small but meaningful gestures of love into your daily life. It will teach you:

- **The Language of Love:** Understanding the different love languages and how to speak them fluently in your relationships.
- **Creative Ideas for Small Gestures:** From handwritten notes to thoughtful surprises, you'll discover a variety of ways to show love without requiring significant effort or expense.
- **The Role of Consistency:** How the regular practice of small gestures creates enduring love and strengthens connections over time.
- **Fostering Self-Love:** Tips for nurturing your own well-being and showing yourself the same kindness and affection you extend to others.

A Foundation for Lasting Connections

Expressing love is an art, and like any art form, it requires practice, observation, and creativity. As you work through this guide, you'll discover that small gestures are not just acts of kindness but also an opportunity to tune into the needs and desires of those you care about. Each thoughtful act, no matter how small, becomes a brushstroke in the masterpiece of your relationships.

So, whether you're crafting a playlist for a friend, surprising your partner with their favorite snack, or simply offering a warm smile to a stranger, remember that these little acts are the heartbeat of love. They may not be grand in scale, but they are monumental in meaning.

Take this journey to explore the profound impact of small but meaningful expressions of love. After all, it's the little things that often mean the most.

Chapter 1: Quick Morning Surprises

Mornings often set the tone for the rest of the day. A small, thoughtful gesture during these early hours can fill the hearts of your loved ones with positivity and warmth, creating a ripple effect that carries throughout their day. Whether you're expressing love to a partner, family member, friend, or even yourself, quick morning surprises can be a powerful way to show care and appreciation.

This chapter explores simple yet impactful ideas for making mornings brighter. These gestures are designed to be time-efficient while carrying the weight of intention and affection.

1.1 The Power of a Thoughtful Wake-Up Call

The way we wake up can influence our mood for the day. Instead of relying on jarring alarm clocks, consider creating a gentle and loving wake-up experience for your loved ones:

- **Personalized Wake-Up Playlist:** Compile a playlist of their favorite songs or calming music. Set it to play softly as they wake up.
- **Whispered Affirmations:** Gently wake them with kind words or affirmations, such as, "Good morning, sunshine. Today is going to be amazing."
- **Morning Aromatherapy:** Use essential oils like lavender or citrus in a diffuser to create a soothing wake-up environment.

1.2 Breakfast with a Loving Twist

Breakfast is often called the most important meal of the day, and it's a perfect opportunity to infuse love into a seemingly routine task.

- **Breakfast in Bed:** Surprise them with a simple tray of their favorite breakfast foods. Even a cup of coffee and toast can feel special when served with love.
- **Hidden Notes:** Slip a handwritten note or a small card with a kind message under their coffee cup, on the fruit bowl, or alongside their cereal box.
- **Custom Creations:** If time permits, create something special, like pancakes shaped as hearts or their initials.

1.3 Acts of Kindness in Preparation

Morning preparations are often hurried, but a little extra effort can go a long way in showing love.

- **Packing Their Bag or Lunch:** If they're heading to work or school, pack their bag or prepare their lunch with an added surprise like a sweet treat or a sticky note that says, "Thinking of you!"
- **Warm Towels:** If they take a morning shower, place their towel in the dryer for a few minutes so it's warm when they step out.
- **Prepped Essentials:** Lay out their favorite outfit, polish their shoes, or ensure their coffee thermos is filled and ready to go.

1.4 Simple Gestures for a Morning Boost

Small, quick gestures can bring unexpected joy to an otherwise routine morning.

- **Compliments:** Start their day with a heartfelt compliment. "You look amazing today!" or "I'm so lucky to have you."
- **Good Morning Texts:** If you're apart, send a thoughtful good morning text filled with love and encouragement.
- **Surprise Flowers:** Place a fresh flower on their bedside table or breakfast plate to bring a smile to their face.

1.5 Self-Love Morning Practices

While it's important to care for others, don't forget about yourself. Practicing self-love in the morning can set a positive tone for your day.

- **Gratitude Journal:** Spend five minutes listing things you're grateful for to cultivate a positive mindset.
- **Morning Affirmations:** Stand in front of the mirror and recite affirmations like, "I am capable, I am loved, and I am ready to embrace today."
- **Pamper Yourself:** Brew your favorite tea or coffee, light a scented candle, and take a few quiet moments to savor your morning.

1.6 Building a Morning Ritual

Creating a morning ritual can make small surprises a consistent part of your day. When practiced regularly, these rituals become a cherished habit that strengthens your relationships.

- **Family Morning Ritual:** Share a quick family tradition, like a group hug, a shared breakfast prayer, or a silly morning dance.
- **Partner Ritual:** Develop a special morning tradition with your partner, like sharing a 5-minute coffee date before leaving for work.
- **Solo Ritual:** If you live alone, make a ritual of sending a quick, loving message to someone you care about to brighten their day and yours.

1.7 The Impact of Quick Morning Surprises

Small morning surprises are not about extravagant efforts; they are about thoughtfulness. These gestures demonstrate that you value and prioritize the happiness of your loved ones, even during the busiest times of the day. Over time, these consistent acts of care build deeper emotional connections and create lasting memories.

Think of each morning as a fresh opportunity to show love. Whether it's through a warm smile, a heartfelt note, or a simple act of kindness, these quick surprises can turn an ordinary morning into an extraordinary one.

By weaving these gestures into your routine, you'll not only brighten someone else's day but also cultivate a sense of joy and fulfillment in your own life. After all, love is in the details—and mornings are the perfect canvas for expressing it.

Chapter 2: Love Notes that Melt Hearts

In a digital age dominated by instant messaging and social media, the charm of a handwritten or thoughtfully crafted love note has not lost its power. Love notes are timeless expressions of affection, capable of evoking deep emotions and strengthening connections in ways that few other gestures can. Whether it's a romantic partner, a close friend, or a family member, a well-written note can convey warmth, gratitude, and appreciation that lingers in the heart for days—or even a lifetime.

This chapter delves into the art of crafting love notes that melt hearts, offering guidance on creating messages that are personal, meaningful, and unforgettable.

2.1 The Timeless Appeal of Love Notes

Why do love notes hold such enduring power? The answer lies in their intimacy. A love note requires time, thought, and effort—qualities that demonstrate genuine care. Unlike fleeting digital messages, a physical note can be cherished, revisited, and even kept as a keepsake.

Love notes also transcend spoken words, allowing the writer to express emotions in a way that feels deeply personal and intentional. The act of writing slows us down, encouraging us to reflect on what we truly feel and want to communicate.

2.2 Types of Love Notes

Love notes can take many forms, each suited to different relationships and occasions. Here are some popular types to inspire you:

1. **Romantic Notes:** Expressing love and affection for a partner.
2. **Affirmation Notes:** Providing encouragement and support to someone who needs it.
3. **Gratitude Notes:** Thanking someone for their kindness or impact on your life.
4. **Celebratory Notes:** Commemorating a special event, such as an anniversary or birthday.
5. **Apology Notes:** Conveying sincerity and a desire to mend a rift.

2.3 How to Write a Love Note That Melts Hearts

Crafting a love note doesn't require poetic talent or grandiose language. What matters most is sincerity. Here's a step-by-step guide to writing a love note that will resonate deeply:

Step 1: Choose the Right Medium

- **Paper or Card:** A handwritten note on a beautiful piece of stationery feels personal and intimate.
- **Digital Message:** While less traditional, a thoughtfully worded email or text can still be meaningful.
- **Creative Surfaces:** Write on a mirror with lipstick, leave a sticky note on their computer, or hide a message in their lunchbox.

Step 2: Begin with a Warm Greeting

Start with an endearing salutation that reflects your relationship:

- Romantic: "My Dearest [Name]," or "To the Love of My Life,"
- Friendly: "Dear [Name]," or "Hey Bestie,"
- Family: "Dearest Mom," or "To My Beloved Sister,"

Step 3: Share Specific Compliments or Memories

Instead of generic praise, mention specific qualities or memories that make them special:

- "I love the way you laugh—it lights up every room you enter."
- "I'll never forget how you stayed by my side when I needed it most."

Step 4: Express Your Feelings

Be vulnerable and honest about how they make you feel:

- "You inspire me to be the best version of myself every day."
- "I'm so grateful to have you in my life; you make everything brighter."

Step 5: End with a Flourish

Close your note with a heartfelt sentiment:

- "Forever yours," or "With all my love,"
- Add a playful or unique touch, such as a doodle, a lipstick kiss, or a sprayed hint of perfume.

2.4 Creative Ideas for Delivering Love Notes

The delivery of your love note can enhance its impact. Here are some creative ways to surprise your recipient:

1. **Hidden Messages:** Slip the note into their pocket, bag, or lunchbox for them to discover later.
2. **Daily Countdown:** Write a series of small notes and leave one for each day leading up to a special occasion.
3. **Puzzle Pieces:** Write the note across several pieces of a puzzle for them to assemble.
4. **Surprise Locations:** Hide a note in unexpected places, such as under their pillow, inside a book they're reading, or taped to the bathroom mirror.
5. **Interactive Notes:** Pair the note with a small gift or token, such as a flower, a piece of chocolate, or a photograph.

2.5 Examples of Heart-Melting Love Notes

Here are some examples to inspire your own writing:

Romantic Love Note:

"My Dearest,

Every day with you feels like a beautiful adventure. Your kindness, strength, and laughter fill my life with joy. Thank you for being my rock, my partner, and my greatest love. I cherish you more than words can say.

Forever yours,

[Your Name]"

Gratitude Note:

"Dear [Name],

I just wanted to take a moment to thank you for always being there for me. Your support means the world to me, and I'm so lucky to have someone as incredible as you in my life. You truly are a blessing.

With gratitude,

[Your Name]"

Encouragement Note:

"Hi [Name],

I know things have been tough lately, but I want you to remember how strong and capable you are. You've overcome so much already, and I believe in you with all my heart. You've got this, and I'm here for you every step of the way.

Love,

[Your Name]"

2.6 Love Notes for Yourself

Don't forget to include yourself in the love note practice. Writing a note to yourself can be a powerful exercise in self-love and affirmation.

Example: "Dear Me,

You've been through so much, yet you keep going with courage and grace. I'm proud of how far you've come and excited for all that lies ahead. You are enough, just as you are, and you deserve all the happiness this world has to offer.

With love,

[Your Name]"

2.7 The Lasting Impact of Love Notes

Love notes are more than just words on paper; they are tangible reminders of affection, appreciation, and connection. They create a sense of intimacy and belonging that is often difficult to achieve through other means. By taking the time to write and deliver a love note, you are giving the recipient a gift that they can hold onto, treasure, and revisit whenever they need a reminder of your care.

Incorporating love notes into your relationships doesn't require much time or effort, but the impact can be profound. Whether it's a romantic partner, a family member, a friend, or yourself, a thoughtfully written note is a small gesture that carries immense meaning. So pick up your pen, let your heart speak, and watch as your words melt hearts and strengthen bonds.

Chapter 3: The Power of Unexpected Compliments

Compliments are gifts wrapped in words—small but potent gestures that have the power to uplift spirits, strengthen relationships, and create moments of pure joy. While compliments are often given in predictable situations, such as during celebrations or after achievements, their true power lies in the element of surprise. Unexpected compliments catch people off guard, making them feel seen, valued, and appreciated in the most genuine way.

In this chapter, we will explore the art of delivering meaningful, unexpected compliments and their profound impact on individuals and relationships.

3.1 Why Compliments Matter

At their core, compliments are affirmations of worth. They acknowledge someone's qualities, efforts, or impact, fostering feelings of connection and self-esteem. Studies in psychology have shown that compliments activate the same reward centers in the brain as receiving tangible rewards, like money or gifts. This makes them not only emotionally significant but also neurologically impactful.

Unexpected compliments go a step further by breaking the routine of daily interactions. They can turn an ordinary moment into something special, creating ripples of positivity that extend far beyond the initial exchange.

3.2 The Anatomy of a Great Compliment

To deliver a compliment that resonates deeply, it must be genuine, specific, and timely. Here's what makes a great compliment:

1. **Authenticity:** A compliment should come from a place of sincerity. Empty flattery can often be detected and may feel insincere.
2. **Specificity:** General praise like "You're amazing!" is nice, but a detailed compliment, such as "I love how you always find creative solutions to challenges," feels more meaningful.
3. **Relevance:** The compliment should align with the recipient's values, efforts, or personality traits to have the greatest impact.

3.3 Crafting Unexpected Compliments

Giving unexpected compliments requires observation, thoughtfulness, and a bit of creativity. Below are strategies to craft compliments that catch people off guard and make a lasting impression:

1. Observe the Little Things

Pay attention to subtle details about the person, such as their habits, style, or personality quirks. Compliments that highlight these often overlooked aspects feel deeply personal.

Examples:

- "I love how you always remember everyone's coffee order—it shows how thoughtful you are."
- "Your laugh is so contagious—it always brightens the room."

2. Acknowledge Effort, Not Just Outcomes

While it's common to praise results, recognizing the hard work and determination someone puts into something can be even more powerful.

Examples:

- "I saw how much effort you put into preparing for that presentation—you did an amazing job."
- "You've been so consistent with your workouts lately—it's inspiring to see your dedication."

3. Compliment Character Traits

Highlighting someone's character traits shows that you value them for who they are, not just what they do.

Examples:

- "You have such a calming presence; it makes people feel at ease around you."
- "Your generosity is incredible—you always find ways to help others."

4. Make It Timely and Contextual

Delivering a compliment during a random moment makes it unexpected and impactful. For example, praising someone while they're in the middle of a task or on a seemingly ordinary day can leave a lasting impression.

Examples:

- "I don't say this enough, but your attention to detail is amazing—it really makes everything you do stand out."
- "I was just thinking about how reliable you are. It's such a comfort to know I can always count on you."

3.4 The Art of Delivering Compliments

How you deliver a compliment is just as important as the compliment itself. The tone, setting, and manner of delivery can amplify its impact:

1. **Choose the Right Moment:** An unexpected compliment works best when it feels natural and not forced. Look for moments when the person isn't expecting praise.
2. **Make Eye Contact:** Eye contact conveys sincerity and helps the recipient feel that your words are genuine.
3. **Speak with Warmth:** Use a kind and enthusiastic tone to emphasize the positive emotions behind your words.
4. **Be Concise:** A short and heartfelt compliment is more impactful than a long-winded one.

3.5 Creative Ways to Deliver Unexpected Compliments

Adding a creative twist to your delivery can make the compliment even more memorable. Here are some ideas:

1. **Compliment Notes:** Write the compliment on a sticky note and leave it in an unexpected place, like their car dashboard, desk, or fridge.
2. **Public Recognition:** Compliment someone in front of others during a meeting, dinner, or gathering.
3. **Compliment Jar:** Create a jar filled with small notes, each containing a compliment. Let them pick one at random when they need a boost.
4. **Text Messages:** Send a heartfelt compliment via text during a random part of the day.
5. **Random Acts of Praise:** While walking together or during a casual conversation, drop a compliment that feels completely spontaneous.

3.6 Compliments for Different Relationships

For Romantic Partners:

Compliments in romantic relationships help keep the spark alive and reinforce feelings of love and attraction.

- "You always know how to make me smile—it's one of my favorite things about you."
- "The way you handled that stressful situation was amazing. You're so strong."

For Friends:

Friends often uplift each other, but unexpected compliments can deepen the bond.

- "You're one of the most loyal people I've ever met—I'm so lucky to have you as a friend."
- "Your creativity blows me away. You have such a unique way of looking at the world."

For Family Members:

Complimenting family members fosters gratitude and strengthens familial ties.

- "You've always been my biggest supporter—I'm so thankful for you."
- "The way you take care of everyone is incredible. You have such a big heart."

For Colleagues:
Compliments in professional settings boost morale and create positive work environments.

- "Your presentation today was outstanding—it's clear how much effort you put into it."
- "You're always so organized and on top of things. It's inspiring to work with you."

3.7 The Ripple Effect of Compliments
Unexpected compliments not only brighten someone's day but also create a ripple effect. When someone receives a compliment, they're more likely to pass that positivity on to others, fostering an environment of kindness and appreciation. Additionally, giving compliments strengthens the bond between the giver and the recipient, creating a cycle of mutual goodwill.

3.8 Encouraging a Culture of Compliments
Make compliment-giving a regular habit in your personal and professional life. By practicing observation and gratitude, you can find countless opportunities to uplift those around you. Over time, you'll notice a shift in your relationships and the overall atmosphere of your interactions.

Conclusion
Unexpected compliments are more than just words—they are acts of love, kindness, and recognition. They have the power to transform ordinary interactions into moments of connection and joy. By learning to craft and deliver thoughtful compliments, you can make a lasting impact on the people in your life while fostering deeper, more meaningful relationships.

So, start looking for the little things worth praising. You might be surprised by how much happiness a few well-chosen words can bring. After all, the most beautiful things in life are often the simplest—and compliments are no exception.

Chapter 4: Last-Minute Gift Ideas for Busy Days

Life often moves at a frenetic pace, and even the most organized among us can find ourselves scrambling for a thoughtful gift at the last minute. Whether it's a forgotten birthday, an unexpected celebration, or a gesture of appreciation, last-minute gifting doesn't have to feel rushed or thoughtless. With a little creativity and resourcefulness, you can give meaningful presents that show how much you care, even on your busiest days.

This chapter will guide you through a variety of quick yet thoughtful gift ideas, categorized for different recipients and occasions. From heartfelt DIY options to convenient store-bought solutions, these ideas will help you become a master of meaningful last-minute gifting.

4.1 The Art of Last-Minute Gifting

A great last-minute gift doesn't have to be extravagant or expensive. What matters most is the thought behind it. To achieve this, focus on three key principles:

1. **Personalization:** Tailor the gift to the recipient's preferences, hobbies, or needs.
2. **Presentation:** A well-packaged gift can elevate even the simplest items.
3. **Timeliness:** Choose something that suits the occasion and feels relevant.

4.2 Quick and Thoughtful DIY Gift Ideas

Handmade gifts are a great way to show you care, even if you're short on time. These ideas are easy to create but carry a personal touch that makes them special.

1. Jar of Gratitude

- **What You'll Need:** A clean jar, small slips of paper, and a pen.
- **How to Make It:** Write down reasons why you appreciate the recipient on the slips of paper and fill the jar. Decorate the jar with a ribbon or label.
- **Why It Works:** It's heartfelt, unique, and a reminder of how much they mean to you.

2. Personalized Recipe Booklet

- **What You'll Need:** Index cards or printed paper, a hole punch, and ribbon or binder clips.
- **How to Make It:** Compile a few of your favorite recipes, especially ones you know they'll love, and assemble them into a booklet.
- **Why It Works:** It's practical and personal, especially for food enthusiasts.

3. Customized Playlist

- **What You'll Need:** Access to a music streaming service and knowledge of their taste in music.
- **How to Make It:** Create a playlist of songs that remind you of them, or pick tracks for a specific theme, like relaxation or motivation. Share the link with a note.
- **Why It Works:** It's thoughtful and easy to execute in minutes.

4. Framed Photo or Quote

- **What You'll Need:** A photo or printout of a meaningful quote, and a frame.
- **How to Make It:** Choose a photo of a shared memory or a quote they'd love, and frame it.
- **Why It Works:** It's personal and can be displayed as a cherished keepsake.

4.3 Store-Bought Solutions That Feel Thoughtful

If you don't have time to make a gift, there are plenty of quick store-bought options that can still convey thoughtfulness.

1. Gift Cards with a Twist

- **What to Do:** Choose a gift card for their favorite store, restaurant, or streaming service. Pair it with a handwritten note explaining why you chose it.
- **Why It Works:** It's versatile and shows you considered their preferences.

2. Specialty Foods or Treats

- **What to Do:** Pick up a box of gourmet chocolates, a bottle of wine, or a selection of artisanal snacks.
- **Why It Works:** Food is universally appreciated and can be enjoyed immediately.

3. Personalized Calendars or Journals

- **What to Do:** Buy a high-quality journal, calendar, or planner. Include a pen or bookmark for an added touch.
- **Why It Works:** It's practical and encourages creativity or organization.

4. Flower Arrangements

- **What to Do:** Grab a bouquet of fresh flowers or a small potted plant from a grocery store or florist.
- **Why It Works:** Flowers brighten any occasion and add a personal touch to the gesture.

4.4 Experience-Based Gifts

Gifts don't always have to be tangible. Experiences can create lasting memories and require minimal preparation.

1. A Surprise Outing

- **What to Do:** Plan a visit to their favorite cafe, park, or local attraction.
- **Why It Works:** It's spontaneous and offers quality time together.

2. At-Home Spa Kit

- **What to Do:** Put together a quick kit with items like face masks, bath salts, and a scented candle.
- **Why It Works:** It promotes relaxation and shows you care about their well-being.

3. Online Classes or Subscriptions

- **What to Do:** Purchase access to an online course, subscription box, or streaming service they'll enjoy.
- **Why It Works:** It's thoughtful and tailored to their interests.

4.5 Gifts for Specific Occasions
Birthdays

- A small cake or cupcakes with a personalized message.
- A handwritten letter reflecting on a favorite memory from the past year.

Anniversaries

- A framed map or print of where you first met or a significant location.
- A set of scented candles for a romantic evening.

Thank You Gifts

- A basket of fresh fruit or baked goods.
- A small notebook with a note: "Because you make life sweeter, here's a place to jot down sweet memories."

Get Well Soon

- A care package with herbal teas, cozy socks, and a book or magazine.
- A puzzle or coloring book to help them pass the time.

4.6 Creative Gift Wrapping for Last-Minute Presents

Even the simplest gift can feel special with creative packaging. If you're in a hurry, here are some quick yet charming wrapping ideas:

- **Brown Paper and Twine:** Use kraft paper with a piece of twine or ribbon for a rustic and elegant look.
- **Fabric Wrap:** Use a scarf or piece of fabric to wrap the gift, which doubles as part of the present.
- **Repurposed Materials:** Decorate a plain gift bag with doodles, stickers, or stamps for a personal touch.

4.7 Emergency Gift Stash

To avoid future last-minute stress, consider keeping an emergency stash of versatile gifts. Here are some items to stock:

- Gift cards for popular stores or online platforms.
- High-quality chocolates, wine, or tea.
- Blank greeting cards.
- Small candles, journals, or photo frames.

4.8 The Thought That Counts

Ultimately, the thoughtfulness behind your gift is what truly matters. Even if it's purchased or prepared at the last minute, a gift that reflects the recipient's personality, interests, or needs will always feel special. Focus on sincerity and creativity, and the recipient will feel the love and effort behind your gesture.

Conclusion

Last-minute gifting doesn't have to be stressful or impersonal. With a little ingenuity and intention, you can create meaningful moments through your gifts, no matter how short the time frame. Whether it's a DIY creation, a store-bought treasure, or an experience to share, the options in this chapter provide a toolkit for busy days. Remember, the best gifts come from the heart—and with the right approach, even a quick gesture can leave a lasting impression.

Chapter 5: Creating Magical Evenings in 5 Minutes

Evenings are a time to unwind, reconnect, and set the tone for a peaceful close to the day. Whether you're aiming to surprise a partner, uplift a friend, bond with family, or treat yourself, creating a magical evening doesn't have to involve hours of preparation or elaborate plans. With just five minutes and a sprinkle of intention, you can transform an ordinary evening into something truly special.

This chapter explores quick yet meaningful ways to create magical evenings that strengthen bonds, foster joy, and leave lasting memories.

5.1 The Ingredients of a Magical Evening

Creating a magical evening doesn't require expensive items or grand gestures. It's about evoking feelings of comfort, connection, and delight. Here are the key elements:

1. **Atmosphere:** The right setting can instantly elevate the mood.
2. **Intentionality:** Small, thoughtful details make all the difference.
3. **Connection:** The evening should bring people closer, whether through conversation, shared activities, or quiet companionship.

5.2 Setting the Mood in Minutes

A captivating atmosphere sets the stage for a magical evening. Here are quick ways to transform your space:

1. Dim the Lights and Add Warm Lighting

- Use candles, fairy lights, or a lamp with a soft bulb to create a cozy glow.
- If you're short on supplies, simply drape a scarf over a lampshade for instant ambiance (ensure it's heat-safe).

2. Play Background Music

- Select a playlist that suits the mood—relaxing instrumental, romantic tunes, or uplifting beats.
- Music streaming platforms often have curated playlists for evenings, such as "Chill Vibes" or "Romantic Dinner."

3. Use Aromatherapy

- Light a scented candle, burn incense, or use a diffuser with essential oils like lavender, vanilla, or sandalwood to create a calming aroma.

4. Tidy Up Key Spaces

- Focus on decluttering areas where you'll spend the evening, such as the living room or dining area. A quick sweep and arranging pillows or throws can make the space feel inviting.

5.3 Magical Evening Ideas for Couples
1. A 5-Minute Romantic Table Setting

- Lay out two plates with folded napkins, even if it's takeout.
- Add a centerpiece: a candle, a small vase with flowers, or even a fruit bowl.
- Write a quick note and place it on their plate: "I'm so grateful for you" or "Here's to a lovely evening together."

2. Stargazing Date

- Grab a blanket, head to the backyard, or open a window with a view of the night sky.
- Share a moment of quiet or talk about your dreams and favorite memories.
- Use a stargazing app to identify constellations for added intrigue.

3. Surprise Sweet Treat

- Heat up a quick dessert, like cookies or brownies, and serve with a scoop of ice cream.
- For an extra touch, drizzle chocolate syrup or sprinkle cinnamon on top.
- Share it together while cuddling on the couch.

5.4 Magical Evening Ideas for Families
1. Impromptu Movie Night

- Let everyone pick a quick snack to share.
- Arrange pillows and blankets to create a cozy "movie fort."
- Dim the lights and start a family favorite movie or show.

2. 5-Minute Gratitude Circle

- Sit together and take turns sharing one thing you're grateful for about the day.
- Write these down on sticky notes and create a "gratitude wall" for the family.
- This simple activity fosters connection and positivity.

3. Flashlight Adventure

- Turn off the lights and let the kids use flashlights to explore the house or backyard.
- Create a quick scavenger hunt with items to find or tasks to complete.

5.5 Magical Evening Ideas for Friends
1. Quick DIY Cocktail or Mocktail Bar

- Set up a small station with soda, juice, and a few garnishes like lemon slices, mint leaves, or sugar for rimming glasses.
- Let everyone customize their drink and toast to friendship.
- Add paper straws or stir sticks for a playful touch.

2. Mini Game Night

- Choose a quick game like charades, Pictionary, or a card game.
- Use a timer or phone app for fast-paced fun.
- If no games are handy, make up a storytelling game where each person adds one sentence to a story.

3. Outdoor Bonfire or Fire Pit Gathering

- Light a small fire if you have a fire pit or portable grill.
- Share stories, roast marshmallows, or simply enjoy the evening breeze.
- No fire pit? Simulate the experience indoors with candles and s'mores in the microwave.

5.6 Magical Evening Ideas for Yourself

1. Spa-Inspired Wind Down

- Run a hot bath or foot soak with Epsom salts and essential oils.
- Light a candle and play calming music or an audiobook.
- End with a quick skincare routine and cozy pajamas.

2. Journaling by Candlelight

- Spend five minutes reflecting on your day in a journal.
- Write about things you're grateful for, dreams you're pursuing, or simply freewrite your thoughts.

3. Indulge in a Mini Treat

- Treat yourself to a small dessert or a favorite beverage.
- Pair it with a book, show, or podcast you've been meaning to enjoy.

5.7 Thoughtful Evening Rituals

Rituals create structure and anticipation, making even short evenings feel meaningful. Consider incorporating one of these quick evening rituals into your routine:

- **Daily Highlight Sharing:** Each person shares their favorite moment of the day during dinner or before bed.
- **Gratitude Lighting:** Light a candle and take a moment to reflect on something you're thankful for before blowing it out.
- **Wind-Down Playlist:** Create a short playlist of calming songs and play it every evening as you relax.

5.8 The Importance of Intentionality

What makes an evening truly magical isn't the time or money spent but the thought and care behind it. When you focus on creating a space where connection and relaxation can flourish, even the simplest gestures take on profound meaning. Whether you're spending the evening with others or by yourself, the key is to be present and embrace the moment.

Conclusion

Creating magical evenings in just five minutes is a practice in mindfulness and creativity. By focusing on atmosphere, connection, and thoughtful details, you can transform any evening into an opportunity to unwind, bond, and celebrate life's simple pleasures. Whether it's a candlelit dinner, a heartfelt conversation, or a solo self-care session, these moments can bring warmth and joy to the end of a busy day.

With these quick and meaningful ideas, you'll always have the tools to make evenings magical—no matter how hectic life may be. Remember, magic isn't in the complexity of what you do; it's in the love and intention you bring to it.

Appendix A: Bonus Ideas for Keeping Romance Alive Every Day

Romance thrives on consistency, creativity, and thoughtfulness. It's not about grand gestures or extravagant displays but the little things you do to show love and appreciation daily. This appendix provides a treasure trove of bonus ideas to help you keep the spark alive in your relationship. These tips are practical, meaningful, and easy to incorporate into your daily routine, ensuring that romance becomes a natural and enduring part of your life together.

A.1 Daily Acts of Love and Appreciation

Small, consistent actions can profoundly impact your relationship by fostering connection and appreciation. Here are ways to express love daily:

1. Morning Messages

- Leave a sticky note with a sweet message on their bathroom mirror or coffee mug.
- Send a text first thing in the morning that says, "Good morning, my love. I hope your day is amazing!"

2. Thoughtful Questions

- Ask about their day in a way that shows genuine interest, such as, "What was the best part of your day?" or "What made you smile today?"
- Revisit memories by asking, "Remember when we first met? What's your favorite memory from that time?"

3. Daily Compliments

- Compliment them on something specific, like their outfit, smile, or the way they handled a situation.
- Rotate between physical compliments, character traits, and acknowledgment of their efforts.

4. Acts of Service

- Do a small chore they dislike, such as folding laundry or washing dishes, without being asked.
- Fill their car with gas, prepare their lunch, or tidy up their workspace as a surprise.

5. End-of-Day Connection

- Set aside five minutes before bed to talk about your day or share something you're grateful for about them.
- Give them a goodnight kiss or a warm hug to close the day on a loving note.

A.2 Keeping Romance Alive Through Spontaneity

Adding elements of surprise to your daily life keeps romance fresh and exciting. Here are some ideas to incorporate spontaneity into your relationship:

1. Random Texts

- Send a text in the middle of the day to say, "I just wanted to let you know how much I love and appreciate you."
- Share a random compliment or a playful inside joke to make them smile.

2. Surprise Dates

- Plan a mini date out of the blue, such as a quick coffee break, a walk in the park, or an ice cream run.
- Turn an ordinary evening into a surprise movie night or picnic in the living room.

3. Unexpected Tokens of Love

- Bring home their favorite snack, drink, or dessert as a surprise treat.
- Leave a flower on their car dashboard, desk, or bedside table for no reason other than to make their day.

4. Capture the Moment

- Snap a candid photo of them doing something they love and send it with a sweet message like, "You're so beautiful when you're focused."
- Write a short poem or note inspired by something they did that day and share it with them.

A.3 Enhancing Physical Affection

Physical affection is a vital part of keeping romance alive. These small but meaningful gestures can strengthen intimacy and closeness:

1. Non-Sexual Touch

- Hold hands while walking or sitting together.
- Gently brush their hair away from their face or touch their shoulder as you pass by.

2. Cuddling and Snuggling

- Spend a few minutes cuddling in the morning or before bed.
- Watch a movie or show while sitting close, wrapped in a blanket.

3. Surprise Kisses

- Kiss their forehead, hand, or cheek when they least expect it.
- Sneak a quick kiss as they're busy doing something—it's a subtle yet intimate way to show affection.

4. Playful Touch

- Give them a light back rub or a playful nudge during a conversation.
- Have fun with small gestures like tickling or playful hugs to keep things lighthearted.

A.4 Shared Activities That Build Connection

Engaging in activities together not only strengthens your bond but also creates lasting memories. Here are ways to stay connected through shared experiences:

1. Cook Together

- Choose a new recipe and work as a team to create a meal.
- Turn cooking into a date by adding music and sipping wine or mocktails as you cook.

2. Create Traditions

- Establish small rituals, like Sunday morning coffee dates or a weekly evening walk.
- Celebrate "just because" days where you do something fun or out of the ordinary together.

3. Learn Something New Together

- Take a class or watch tutorials on something you've both wanted to try, like painting, dancing, or gardening.
- Explore hobbies that interest both of you, such as photography, hiking, or gaming.

4. Exercise or Meditate Together

- Join a fitness class, take a yoga session, or go for a jog together.
- Practice guided meditations or breathing exercises as a way to relax and connect.

A.5 Showing Love in Words

Words are a powerful way to keep romance alive. Use these ideas to express your love through verbal and written communication:

1. Love Letters

- Write them a short love letter every now and then, even if it's just a few lines.
- Leave a longer letter for anniversaries, birthdays, or special moments to reflect on your journey together.

2. Appreciation Journal

- Keep a shared journal where you write down something you appreciate about each other each day or week.
- Share it periodically to remind yourselves of the love and gratitude you share.

3. Words of Encouragement

- Remind them of their strengths and abilities, especially during tough times.
- Say, "I'm proud of you," "I believe in you," or "You inspire me" whenever the moment calls for it.

A.6 Infusing Romance Into the Everyday

Romance doesn't always have to be a separate event or activity—it can be seamlessly woven into your daily routines:

1. Celebrate Small Wins

- Acknowledge little achievements, like finishing a task or making it through a tough day, with words of encouragement or a small treat.

2. Turn Chores Into Quality Time

- Do household tasks together while chatting or playing music.
- Turn folding laundry or washing dishes into an opportunity to laugh and share stories.

3. Create Mini Adventures

- Run errands together and add a fun twist, like stopping for a coffee or picking out a new snack to try.
- Explore a nearby park, new store, or local event for a quick change of pace.

A.7 Nurturing Emotional Intimacy

Emotional intimacy is the foundation of a lasting romance. Here's how to nurture it every day:

1. Practice Active Listening

- Give them your full attention during conversations—no phones, no distractions.
- Reflect back what they say to show you're engaged and truly hearing them.

2. Share Vulnerabilities

- Open up about your feelings, hopes, and fears to foster a deeper connection.
- Create a safe space for them to share without judgment or interruption.

3. Celebrate "Us" Moments

- Take time to reflect on your relationship and express gratitude for the journey you're on together.
- Look through old photos or revisit places that hold special memories.

Conclusion

Keeping romance alive every day doesn't require elaborate plans or expensive gestures. The key lies in the small, thoughtful actions that communicate love, appreciation, and connection consistently. By incorporating these bonus ideas into your routine, you can nurture a relationship that feels vibrant, exciting, and deeply fulfilling.

Remember, the essence of romance is about showing your partner that they are loved and valued. Through intentionality, creativity, and a willingness to put effort into the relationship, you'll create a bond that grows stronger with each passing day.

<u>Message from the Author:</u>

I hope you enjoyed this book, I love astrology and knew there was not a book such as this out on the shelf. I love metaphysical items as well. Please check out my other books:

-Life of Government Benefits

-My life of Hell

-My life with Hydrocephalus

-Red Sky

-World Domination:Woman's rule

-World Domination:Woman's Rule 2: The War

-Life and Banishment of Apophis: book 1

-The Kidney Friendly Diet

-The Ultimate Hemp Cookbook

-Creating a Dispensary(legally)

-Cleanliness throughout life: the importance of showering from childhood to adulthood.

-Strong Roots: The Risks of Overcoddling children

-Hemp Horoscopes: Cosmic Insights and Earthly Healing

- Celestial Hemp Navigating the Zodiac: Through the Green Cosmos

-Astrological Hemp: Aligning The Stars with Earth's Ancient Herb

-The Astrological Guide to Hemp: Stars, Signs, and Sacred Leaves

-Green Growth: Innovative Marketing Strategies for your Hemp Products and Dispensary

-Cosmic Cannabis

-Astrological Munchies

-Henry The Hemp

-Zodiacal Roots: The Astrological Soul Of Hemp

- **Green Constellations: Intersection of Hemp and Zodiac**

-Hemp in The Houses: An astrological Adventure Through The Cannabis Galaxy

-Galactic Ganja Guide

Heavenly Hemp

Zodiac Leaves

Doctor Who Astrology

Cannastrology

Stellar Satvias and Cosmic Indicas

Celestial Cannabis: A Zodiac Journey

AstroHerbology: The Sky and The Soil: Volume 1

AstroHerbology:Celestial Cannabis:Volume 2

Cosmic Cannabis Cultivation

The Starry Guide to Herbal Harmony: Volume 1

The Starry Guide to Herbal Harmony: Cannabis Universe: Volume 2

Yugioh Astrology: Astrological Guide to Deck, Duels and more

Nightmare Mansion: Echoes of The Abyss

Nightmare Mansion 2: Legacy of Shadows

Nightmare Mansion 3: Shadows of the Forgotten

Nightmare Mansion 4: Echoes of the Damned

The Life and Banishment of Apophis: Book 2

Nightmare Mansion: Halls of Despair

Healing with Herb: Cannabis and Hydrocephalus

Planetary Pot: Aligning with Astrological Herbs: Volume 1

Fast Track to Freedom: 30 Days to Financial Independence Using AI, Assets, and Agile Hustles

Cosmic Hemp Pathways

How to Become Financially Free in 30 Days: 10,000 Paths to Prosperity

Zodiacal Herbage: Astrological Insights: Volume 1

Nightmare Mansion: Whispers in the Walls

The Daleks Invade Atlantis

Henry the hemp and Hydrocephalus

10X The Kidney Friendly Diet

Cannabis Universe: Adult coloring book

Hemp Astrology: The Healing Power of the Stars

Zodiacal Herbage: Astrological Insights: Cannabis Universe: Volume 2

<u>Planetary Pot: Aligning with Astrological Herbs: Cannabis Universes: Volume 2</u>

Doctor Who Meets the Replicators and SG-1: The Ultimate Battle for Survival

Nightmare Mansion: Curse of the Blood Moon

<u>The Celestial Stoner: A Guide to the Zodiac</u>

Cosmic Pleasures: Sex Toy Astrology for Every Sign

Hydrocephalus Astrology: Navigating the Stars and Healing Waters

Lapis and the Mischievous Chocolate Bar

Celestial Positions: Sexual Astrology for Every Sign

Apophis's Shadow Work Journal: : A Journey of Self-Discovery and Healing

Kinky Cosmos: Sexual Kink Astrology for Every Sign

Digital Cosmos: The Astrological Digimon Compendium

Stellar Seeds: The Cosmic Guide to Growing with Astrology

Apophis's Daily Gratitude Journal

Cat Astrology: Feline Mysteries of the Cosmos

The Cosmic Kama Sutra: An Astrological Guide to Sexual Positions

Unleash Your Potential: A Guided Journal Powered by AI Insights

Whispers of the Enchanted Grove

Cosmic Pleasures: An Astrological Guide to Sexual Kinks

369, 12 Manifestation Journal

Whisper of the nocturne journal(blank journal for writing or drawing)

The Boogey Book

Locked In Reflection: A Chastity Journey Through Locktober

Generating Wealth Quickly:

How to Generate $100,000 in 24 Hours

Star Magic: Harness the Power of the Universe

The Flatulence Chronicles: A Fart Journal for Self-Discovery

The Doctor and The Death Moth

Seize the Day: A Personal Seizure Tracking Journal

The Ultimate Boogeyman Safari: A Journey into the Boogie World and Beyond

Whispers of Samhain: 1,000 Spells of Love, Luck, and Lunar Magic: Samhain Spell Book

Apophis's guides:

Witch's Spellbook Crafting Guide for Halloween

<u>Frost & Flame: The Enchanted Yule Grimoire of 1000 Winter Spells</u>

<u>The Ultimate Boogey Goo Guide & Spooky Activities for Halloween Fun</u>

Harmony of the Scales: A Libra's Spellcraft for Balance and Beauty

The Enchanted Advent: 36 Days of Christmas Wonders

Nightmare Mansion: The Labyrinth of Screams

Harvest of Enchantment: 1,000 Spells of Gratitude, Love, and Fortune for Thanksgiving

The Boogey Chronicles: A Journal of Nightly Encounters and Shadowy Secrets

The 12 Days of Financial Freedom: A Step-by-Step Christmas Countdown to Transform Your Finances

Sigil of the Eternal Spiral Blank Journal

A Christmas Feast: Timeless Recipes for Every Meal

Holiday Stress-Free Solutions: A Survival Guide to Thriving During the Festive Season

Yu-Gi-Oh! Holiday Gifting Mastery: The Ultimate Guide for Fans and Newcomers Alike

Holiday Harmony: A Hydrocephalus Survival Guide for the Festive Season

Celestial Craft: The Witch's Almanac for 2025 – A Cosmic Guide to Manifestations, Moons, and Mystical Events

Doctor Who: The Toymaker's Winter Wonderland

Tulsa King Unveiled: A Thrilling Guide to Stallone's Mafia Masterpiece

Pendulum Craft: A Complete Guide to Crafting and Using Personalized Divination Tools

Nightmare Mansion: Santa's Eternal Eve

Starlight Noel: A Cosmic Journey through Christmas Mysteries

The Dark Architect: Unlocking the Blueprint of Existence

Surviving the Embrace: The Ultimate Guide to Encounters with The Hugging Molly

The Enchanted Codex: Secrets of the Craft for Witches, Wiccans, and Pagans

Harvest of Gratitude: A Complete Thanksgiving Guide

Yuletide Essentials: A Complete Guide to an Authentic and Magical Christmas

Celestial Smokes: A Cosmic Guide to Cigars and Astrology

Living in Balance: A Comprehensive Survival Guide to Thriving with Diabetes Insipidus

Cosmic Symbiosis: The Venom Zodiac Chronicles

The Cursed Paw of Ambition

Cosmic Symbiosis: The Astrological Venom Journal

Celestial Wonders Unfold: A Stargazer's Guide to the Cosmos (2024-2029)

The Ultimate Black Friday Prepper's Guide: Mastering Shopping Strategies and Savings

Cosmic Sales: The Astrological Guide to Black Friday Shopping

Legends of the Corn Mother and Other Harvest Myths

Whispers of the Harvest: The Corn Mother's Journal

The Evergreen Spellbook

The Doctor Meets the Boogeyman

The White Witch of Rose Hall's SpellBook

The Gingerbread Golem's Shadow: A Study in Sweet Darkness

The Gingerbread Golem Codex: An Academic Exploration of Sweet Myths

The Gingerbread Golem Grimoire: Sweet Magicks and Spells for the Festive Witch

The Curse of the Gingerbread Golem

10-minute Christmas Crafts for kids

<u>Christmas Crisis Solutions: The Ultimate Last-Minute Survival Guide</u>

Gingerbread Golem Recipes: Holiday Treats with a Magical Twist

The Infinite Key: Unlocking Mystical Secrets of the Ages

Enchanted Yule: A Wiccan and Pagan Guide to a Magical and Memorable Season

Dinosaurs of Power: Unlocking Ancient Magick

Astro-Dinos: The Cosmic Guide to Prehistoric Wisdom

Gallifrey's Yule Logs: A Festive Doctor Who Cookbook

The Dino Grimoire: Secrets of Prehistoric Magick

The Gift They Never Knew They Needed

The Gingerbread Golem's Culinary Alchemy: Enchanting Recipes for a Sweetly Dark Feast

A Time Lord Christmas: Holiday Adventures with the Doctor

Krampusproofing Your Home: Defensive Strategies for Yule

Silent Frights: A Collection of Christmas Creepypastas to Chill Your Bones

Santa Raptor's Jolly Carnage: A Dino-Claus Christmas Tale

Prehistoric Palettes: A Dino Wicca Coloring Journey

The Christmas Wishkeeper Chronicles

The Micro-Mastery Method: Transform Your Skills in Just Minutes a Day

Reclaiming Time: How to Live More by Doing Less

Chronovore: The Eternal Nexus

The Mind Reset: Unlocking Your Inner Peace in a Chaotic World

Confidence Code: Building Unshakable Self-Belief

Baby the Vampire Terrier

Baby the Vampire Terrier's Christmas Adventure

Celestial Streams: The Content Creator's Astrology Manual

The Wealth Whisperer: Unlocking Abundance with Everyday Actions

The Energy Equation: Maximize Your Output Without Burning Out

The Happiness Algorithm: Science-Backed Steps to Joyful Living

Stress-Free Success: Achieving Goals Without Anxiety

Mindful Wealth: The New Blueprint for Financial Freedom

The Festive Flavors of New Year: A Culinary Celebration

The Master's Gambit: Keys of Eternal Power

Shadowed Secrets: Groundhog Day Mysteries

Beneath the Burrow: Lessons from the Groundhog

Spring's Whispers: The Groundhog's Prediction

The Limitless Mindset: Unlock Your Untapped Potential

The Focus Funnel: How to Cut Through Chaos and Get Results

Bold Moves: Building Courage to Live on Your Terms

The Daily Shift: Simple Practices for Lasting Transformation

The Quarter-Life Reset: Thriving in Your 20s and 30s

The Art of Shadowplay: Building Your Own Personal Myth

The Eternal Loop: Finding Purpose in Repetition

Burrowing Wisdom: Life Lessons from the Groundhog

Shadow Work: A Groundhog Day Perspective

If you want solar for your home go here: https://www.harborso-lar.live/apophisenterprises/

Get Some Tarot cards: https://www.makeplayingcards.com/sell/
apophis-occult-shop

Get some shirts: https://www.bonfire.com/store/apophis-shirt-emporium/

<u>**Instagrams:**</u>
@apophis_enterprises,
@apophisbookemporium,
@apophisscardshop
Twitter: @apophisenterpr1
Tiktok:@apophisenterprise
Youtube: @sg1fan23477, @FiresideRetreatKingdom
Hive: @sg1fan23477
CheeLee: @SG1fan23477
Podcast: Apophis Chat Zone: https://open.spotify.com/show/5zXbrCLEV2xzCp8ybrfHsk?si=fb4d4fdbdce44dec

Newsletter: https://apophiss-newsletter-27c897.beehiiv.com/

If you want to support me or see posts of other projects that I have come over to: **buymeacoffee.com/mpetchinskg**
I post there daily several times a day

Get your Dinowicca or Christmas themed digital products, especially Santa Raptor songs and other musics. Here: **https://sg1fan23477.gumroad.com**

Apophis Yuletide Digital has not only digital Christmas items, but it will have all things with Dinowicca as well as other Digital products.